EISENSTAEDT

MARTHA'S VINEYARD

EISENSTAEDT

MARTHA'S VINEYARD

Text by Polly Burroughs

Oxmoor
House

SOUTH BEACH, CHILMARK

For all those at Slim Chance Farm who have brought such joy to everyone—Rick, Nancy, Nicholas, and Scup

I would like to thank Art Railton, former president of the Dukes County Historical Society; Everett Poole of Menemsha; Mrs. Thomas Chirgwin of Edgartown; and Ralph Graves, novelist and former managing editor of Life Magazine, *for their most valuable assistance. I am particularly indebted to Richard Reston, editor of the* Vineyard Gazette, *and also to Eulalie Regan, librarian of the* Vineyard Gazette, *for her thoughtfulness and help in providing profiles from the newspaper's archives of the following: Somerset Maugham, Captain Donald Poole, Captain Norman Benson, Napoleon Bonaparte Madison, David Vanderhoop, Manuel Swartz Roberts, Captain Tom Tilton, William Styron, Lillian Hellman, Ruth Gordon, and Thornton Wilder.*

Polly Burroughs

KATHY EISENSTAEDT

This book is dedicated to the memory of my wife, with whom I spent twenty-two summers on the island.

For nearly half a century, I have spent my vacation on Martha's Vineyard, and the photographing I did was purely for my own pleasure. It was while discussing this lifelong affection for the island, its people, and breathtaking beauty with my friend Polly Burroughs, who was particularly interested in the historical value of the thousands of photographs I had taken over the years, that the idea for this book began. I am indebted to Geraldine Howard of Life Picture Service, who did the tremendous job of editing the volume of photographs and worked as liaison with Oxmoor House in having their selections processed at Time-Life Photo Lab. And to the staff of Oxmoor House, my sincere thanks.

Eisenstaedt

Library of Congress Catalog Number: 87-62926
ISBN: 0-8487-1002-9
Manufactured in the United States of America
First Edition

Special thanks to Geraldine Howard, Picture Editor, *Life* Picture Service, for coordinating all photographs and for the biographical information on Alfred Eisenstaedt.

Published by Oxmoor House, Inc.
Book Division of Southern Progress Corporation
P.O. Box 2463, Birmingham, Alabama 35201

Editor-in-Chief: John Logue
Executive Editor: Candace N. Conard
Production Manager: Jerry Higdon
Associate Production Manager: Rick Litton
Art Director: Bob Nance

EISENSTAEDT Martha's Vineyard

Editor: Cecilia C. Robinson
Editorial Assistant: Josie Ellixson Lee
Designer: Carol Middleton
Production Assistant: Theresa L. Beste
Map illustrations: David Morrison

AFTER THE STORM, RAINBOW

(Title page) A rainbow at Lobsterville Beach, taken from across Menemsha Harbor just after a storm.

LOBSTERVILLE

(Contents page) In the late nineteenth century, before Menemsha Harbor's basin was built, the lucrative lobster fishery was located at Lobsterville. It was an active spot during the summer months, with boathouses lining the shore, fishing gear and lobster pots strewn about, even a small general store. Smacks arrived daily from New York City to purchase lobsters for five cents each. Besides a public beach, the area now contains a bird sanctuary for nesting terns.

CONTENTS

ALFRED EISENSTAEDT

Pioneering photojournalist Alfred Eisenstaedt was born in Dirschau, West Prussia (now Tczew, Poland), in 1898, and his family moved to Berlin when he was still a child. An uncle gave him his first camera, an Eastman folding camera No. 3, in his early teens, but he did not consider photography as a profession for many years.

At 17, Eisenstaedt's schooling was interrupted when he was drafted into the German army during World War I. He served on the Flanders front, and on April 12, 1918, he sustained shrapnel injuries in both legs during the second western offensive. The only survivor of his artillery battery, Eisenstaedt was sent home to recuperate. It was one year before he was able to walk again unaided, and during his recuperation, his interest in photography was renewed. First on crutches and later on two canes, he began going to museums to study the light and composition in the paintings of the masters. He also studied the work of a man whom he admired, Dr. Erich Salomon, one of the founders of photojournalism and best known for his candid photographs of statesmen and celebrities.

When he recovered from his wounds, Eisenstaedt took a job as a salesman in the retail business, but all his extra time and money went into photography. In 1927, while accompanying his parents to Czechoslovakia on holiday, he made the photograph that would start his career. It was of a woman playing tennis, and he sold it to the illustrated weekly *Der Welt Spiegel* for about $3.00.

In the late 1920s and early 1930s, there were more illustrated magazines in Germany than in any other country, and the editors of these publications fostered the new style of unposed candid photography that Eisenstaedt practiced. Encouraged by the editor to bring in

MENEMSHA HARBOR, 1962
Since 1950, Eisenstaedt ("Eisie" to his friends) has stayed at Menemsha Inn every summer. "I get up at 5:30 in the morning and often go down to Dutcher Dock and photograph. I used my Leica with a 50-mm lens for this picture."

KATHY EISENSTAEDT AT ZACK'S CLIFFS, 1960
*(**Following overleaf**) Each summer Eisie and Kathy would go to the beach to picnic and swim. Kathy is reading here.*

GAY HEAD CLIFFS, 1972
Eisie considers this one of his best photographs of the cliffs; even the clouds cooperated in providing an ideal composition.

more photographs, Eisenstaedt left the retail business and became a freelance photographer working for Pacific and Atlantic Photos. In 1931, the Associated Press took over Pacific and Atlantic Photos, and Eisenstaedt began his association with that agency. About the same time, he first heard of the 35-mm Leica, although it had been invented a few years earlier, and he became skilled in its use. Eisenstaedt's reputation grew as more people came to appreciate his innate skills of a remarkable eye, lightning reflexes, and an instant sense of composition. He was among the few allowed to be present in 1933 for the first meeting of Hitler and Mussolini. He continued to cover Hitler's rise to power, and in 1935, he photographed a notable series on Ethiopia documenting that country's preparations for war against the Italians.

The ascendancy of Hitler caused many of Germany's publications to fold, and most of the photographers left for other European countries and the United States. Eisenstaedt came to America with

GAY HEAD, 1965

his widowed mother in 1935, and he was soon hired by Henry Luce along with Margaret Bourke-White, Thomas McAvoy, and Peter Stackpole to work on the secret "Project X." On November 23, 1936, that project became *Life* Magazine; the first issue contained five of Eisenstaedt's pictures, and the second issue featured one of his pictures on the cover.

Eisenstaedt was not yet a citizen of the United States when World War II began, so his assignments continued to be limited to America. On V-J Day in 1945, he took the picture for which he is most famous, a sailor kissing a nurse in Times Square.

By the end of the war, Eisenstaedt had attained American citizenship, and he was assigned to cover Japan after her defeat. In addition to photographs of Emperor Hirohito and General Hideki Tojo, he captured on film the devastation the bomb had caused to the land and to the people of Japan.

In 1947, Eisenstaedt met the woman who would become his wife, Kathy Kaye. He recalls, "Kathy had the most beautiful voice. That is what I noticed first about her." Originally from South Africa, Miss Kaye was living with her sister, Lucille Kaye, in New York City at the time. Eisenstaedt and Kathy Kaye were married in 1949; she is now deceased.

From the 1950s to the present, Eisenstaedt's assignments have been many and varied. He has made outstanding portraits of kings, dictators, literary figures, and motion picture stars, but he has also sensitively photographed ordinary people in workday situations. Over the years, Eisenstaedt has received numerous prestigious awards for photographic achievement, including the National Press Photographers Association Joseph A. Sprague Memorial Award; International Understanding Award for Outstanding Achievement in Photography; Culture Prize in Photography from the German Society of Photographers, Cologne; Clifton C. Edom Award for Photographic Achievement from Kappa Alpha Mu National Photojournalism Fraternity; and Distinction in Photography as one of the world's ten great photographers in an international poll conducted by *Popular Photography*. He also has written twelve books about his life and work, among them *Witness to Our Time, The Eye of Eisenstaedt, Witness to Nature,* and *Album: People—Guide to Photography.*

SURF WITH FOAM, SOUTH BEACH, 1955

"I love this picture—the beautiful shape. You know, every wave is different, and I stood there a long time waiting for this one. The wave and foam pattern, the shiny wet sand, and the white dunes in the background make a wonderful composition. I had to make sure there were no footprints, nothing to spoil the graceful line of that receding wave. A yellow filter was used with my Leica and 35-mm lens to darken the sky, to make the contrast with the white foam. Without strong sunlight and a deep blue sky, this picture would not have been possible." It is one of Eisie's favorite photographs.

Characterizing his work, Eisenstaedt once said, "The photojournalist's job is to find and catch the storytelling moment." Ralph Graves, novelist and former managing editor of *Life* Magazine, has observed, "Quite aside from his visual and technical skills, Eisie has special qualities that set him apart. To Eisenstaedt, everything is interesting and therefore potentially a picture. Because of this intense curiosity, he finds pictures that other photographers overlook. What he likes best is to see life unrolling right in front of his eyes, the faster and the livelier the better, and Eisie right there with a 35-mm camera in his hands to get it all down. All of it."

Today Eisenstaedt, or "Eisie" as he is affectionately known by his friends, continues to work with the same enthusiasm that he first brought to photography. This collection of photographs, with the exception of a few that were published in *Life* and *People* magazines, consists of those taken solely for Eisie's personal pleasure. Of all the places around the globe he has lived in and visited, Eisie has chosen Martha's Vineyard for the past fifty years as his haven for relaxation after demanding photography assignments and hectic world travel. Here he can stop for a while to listen, watch, and commune with the natural environment he loves, and fortunately a part of Eisie moves him to record these occasions he enjoys so much. Walking the Vineyard's beaches summer after summer with his wife, Kathy, and continuing to come after her death, he has paused to focus one of the cameras that are always with him and capture a scene others can enjoy long after the moment has passed. He has never tired of the extraordinary life he has lived through the lens.

SUMMER, GAY HEAD, 1971

"I was standing on the cliffs admiring the view when I spotted this young person standing on the rocks down below with a companion and waited for the right moment to photograph." The ocean was shimmering in the afternoon sun.

SKATE FISH EGGSHELLS

Rarely does Eisie pose a picture, preferring nature as he finds it. But when he saw these dried skate fish eggshells, he felt compelled to create the composition.

"I posed this one. I couldn't resist—they reminded me so much of people dancing. I arranged them in a continuous winding line, and the picture would not have worked if the sand was disturbed, so I had to smooth it over. I had to lie down to photograph from a low viewpoint, which provided the right perspective. It took several hours to get it right. I used a Nikon camera and 50-mm lens, plus a polarizing filter to darken the sky, separating it from the white sand."

MARTHA'S VINEYARD

A light sou'wester was kicking up gentle whitecaps on that bright blue July day in 1937 when Roy Larsen, publisher of *Life* Magazine and vice president of Time Inc., nudged his speedboat alongside the town dock in New London, Connecticut. Alfred Eisenstaedt was waiting at the pier and jumped aboard.

Eisie had an assignment to do a story about the island of Martha's Vineyard for *Life*. There had been a ferry strike and no boats were running from Cape Cod to the Vineyard, so Eisie had taken the train down from New York City to this seaport town where Larsen had agreed to meet him. It was a long trip to the island, but with both engines wide open and calm seas, they sped across Rhode Island Sound. They made good time as they passed the cliffs at Gay Head, rounded the eastern end of the island, and entered Vineyard Sound, finally coming into Edgartown Harbor. Larsen dropped Eisie off at the Edgartown Yacht Club's pier and headed off to Nantucket Island, where he had a summer home for many years.

The Edgartown waterfront was teeming with midsummer activity. Near Eldridge's fish market, sparks lit up the darkened interior of Orin Norton's shop as the old blacksmith hammered away on some hot metal. Fishing boats and pleasure boats were tied up alongside the adjoining piers of weathered boathouses. The ground was covered with bright white crushed scallop shells. A block up from the waterfront was the inn where Eisie had booked reservations for five days. It proved to be an unusual assignment because it would have such a profound effect on the rest of his life.

"Everything was so new to me. It was fascinating—unbelievable," Eisie recalls of that first visit to the island. "I had only been in America two years." He looked forward to the Vineyard assignment

LADIES STROLLING IN MENEMSHA, 1937
Eisie spotted these fashionable ladies on his first visit to Martha's Vineyard over fifty years ago.

EDGARTOWN HARBOR, 1969
Eisie took this photograph from the deck at the top of the town dock, which affords a beautiful view of both the inner and outer harbor. Chappaquiddick Island is in the background.

CHURCH'S MARKET, OAK BLUFFS, 1937

with a youthful sense of wonder and excitement. Intensely curious
about everything, Eisie was enthralled by the light and color and
especially the scenery in the sparsely settled up-island areas.

There were few paved roads in those days and no electricity in Gay
Head, and telephones were all on party lines. There were far fewer
summer visitors in those days; fishing and farming played a much
larger role in island life then than it does today. Vineyard Haven was
still a busy commercial port with steamers, barges, tugs, and fishing
boats filling the harbor; Oak Bluffs bustled with holiday frivolity, its
theaters featuring *Tarzan* and the films of Laurel and Hardy; and in
Edgartown, which was becoming a large summer resort, the New
York Yacht Club was due in on its annual cruise. Some of Edgartown's inns featured afternoon tea in their lovely gardens, and these
"tea gardens" were very popular with summer vacationers. A local
dry goods store featured sneakers for $1.29 a pair that summer, men's
shirts were $1.00 each, and three heads of lettuce cost $.25.

Artists and intellectuals were attracted to the up-island area not
only for economic reasons but also for its unspoiled beauty. Jackson
Pollock was visiting Thomas Hart Benton that summer, staying in

SOUTH SHORE, GAY HEAD
The Atlantic Ocean runs all along the south side of Martha's Vineyard for twenty miles, from Chappaquiddick to Gay Head. Large and small windswept dunes line the shore, and fingerlike ponds and coves jut in from the sea. This is typical of the many sandy dirt roads that wind through the beach grass and lead down to the ocean.

Benton's chicken coop; James Cagney asked Captain Zebulon Tilton if he could go along when Zeb sailed his schooner over to Nantucket with a load of firewood; and Roger Baldwin, one of the founders of the American Civil Liberties Union, hosted daily nude-bathing picnics at Windy Gates Farm, his place on the south shore.

The western end of the island, which includes the towns of West Tisbury, Chilmark, and Gay Head, contained communities devoted primarily to fishing and farming, ways of life that were sometimes harsh but appealed to many of these independent Yankees. Their ancestors had learned much about fishing and farming from the Native Americans of the island, and the history of these early white settlers and that of the Indians are closely intertwined.

ROSES, CHILMARK

Roses thrive everywhere on the island, and the evening mistings are wonderful for the plants. In the down-island towns, carefully pruned climbers decorate white picket fences and flourish in formal gardens, while in the more rural areas, ramblers tumble over stone walls, their fragrance tingeing the salt air.

GIANT OAK TREE, NORTH TISBURY, 1969

"It's not so easy to photograph this tree as it looks. If I went any closer, it would spoil the composition. The object was to keep the right side in balance with the left. I used my Nikon with a 35-mm lens." Children used to climb and swing on this ancient tree. Since this was taken, the branches have become so heavy some are touching the ground.

The Indians on the island had taken their living from the land and sea for centuries before white men, led by English explorer Captain Bartholomew Gosnold, came in 1602. It is believed Gosnold may have named the island in honor of either his daughter or mother-in-law and also for the plentiful grapevines he found there.

In October of 1641, Thomas Mayhew of Watertown, Massachusetts, and his son, Thomas Jr., purchased Martha's Vineyard, Nantucket Island, and the Elizabeth Islands from two English noblemen who had conflicting grants to the area. The following year, Thomas Jr. arrived with a group of colonists and chose Edgartown, which they called Great Harbor, for the first white settlement on the island.

The original settlers found the Native Americans to be a friendly, peaceful tribe and extremely helpful. The Indians belonged to the Pokanocket Confederacy, a tribe more commonly known as the *Wampanoags* (meaning "Easterners"), and spoke the Algonquian language. Their economy was based on fishing and farming rather than hunting, and they willingly shared their knowledge of taming the wilderness to meet their needs, which consisted of whaling alongshore, gathering wild fruit and harvesting shellfish, seining creeks for herring and planting corn in the spring, fishing for codfish and eels in winter, and shooting wildfowl and upland game birds in fall. The Great Harbor settlement grew slowly; there were eighty-five white settlers on the island in 1660.

Governor Mayhew ruled the island in an autocratic manner, and one of his primary missions was to Christianize the Indians. Three succeeding generations of Mayhews were also deeply involved in this undertaking, earning themselves the title of "Missionary Mayhews." They exercised an important influence over the character and growth of the island. There was never any open hostility between the two groups, although the Indians were exploited and the Mayhews were accused of running a feudal state.

Mayhew may have bought the island, but the white settlers for the most part purchased their land from the Indians, often nudging the natives off the richer lands. The settlers were farmers by heritage, and as other settlements sprang up on the Vineyard, self-sufficient communities developed: mills along the north shore of the island made brick and paint from the clay, others ground corn, and great flocks of sheep provided food and woolen cloth. They evaporated sea water for salt, hunted wild game, and grew their own vegetables. But more and more they looked to the sea and maritime trade, exporting cranberries, salted codfish, and with the growth of the whaling industry, candles and whale oil. Each of the island towns developed its own visual and economic character based on its relationship to the sea, each reaching its peak of prosperity in the mid-nineteenth century. Whaling became Edgartown's principal industry, Vineyard Haven was an important anchorage for New York-to-Maine shipping as well as for those trading with the West Indies, and Oak Bluffs began to develop as a summer resort after its initial development as a Methodist meeting campground.

For over two centuries, nearly every man and boy was lured to the waterfront, where tales of adventure and enticing riches lay at hand.

DUTCHER DOCK, MENEMSHA, 1962

Shipyards, bakeries turning out hardtack, blacksmiths, food shops provisioning the ships, sail lofts, a tannery, and cordwainers were busy supplying the vessels. The majority of Vineyard men either worked in these businesses serving the maritime trade or earned their living as captains and owners or crew members of whaleships, vessels trading with the West Indies, coastwise schooners, fishing boats, and clipper ships.

The discovery of petroleum in 1859 signaled the beginning of the American whaling industry's end, which was rapidly accelerated by the destruction of Yankee whaleships during the Civil War. The completion of the Cape Cod Canal in 1914 coupled with the increasing movement of freight by steamship, train, and truck rather than under sail marked the start of the decline of Vineyard Haven as a commercial port. The era of oar and sail on Martha's Vineyard came to a close.

Gradually the resort business grew, particularly in the towns of Vineyard Haven, Oak Bluffs, and Edgartown, while fishing and farming continued as the main industries of the up-island areas of West Tisbury, Chilmark, and Gay Head. The one exception to this is

CAPTAIN NORMAN G. BENSON, 1971

When Eisie drove up to Captain Benson's white clapboard house on a bluff overlooking Vineyard Sound to photograph, Norman was busy chopping up horseshoe crabs to bait his eel traps out in the sound. A New England Yankee in the finest sense of the term, Norman was one of the most respected and beloved of men—honest, forthright, and a wonderful storyteller. A great family man, Norman instilled in his children the integrity and virtues he had inherited from his whaling and fishing forbears. He was a fisherman all his life and the last one on the Vineyard to earn a living setting out nets alongshore to trap the fish sold to New York's Fulton Street markets. When trap fishing was no longer feasible, Norman went eeling and swordfishing. The small eels he kept in his cellar to sell to the local fishermen, and the large ones he shipped off-island to markets in Boston.

Norman was friendly with Joshua Slocum and put a coat of bottom paint on the thirty-seven-foot sloop Spray *before Slocum made his ill-fated plan to sail to South America.*

CAPTAIN THOMAS TILTON, 1971

One of the island's most able seamen in his day, the late Captain Tom T. Tilton first went trap fishing at the age of twelve and spent his life at sea. A superb boatman, he earned the respect and admiration of all who knew him for his integrity and expertise, whether it was dragging for bottom fish, going offshore for swordfish, or coasting along New England on the Alice S. Wentworth, his uncle Zebulon Tilton's schooner.

Tom posed here in his foul-weather gear for Eisie for a book about Captain Zeb Tilton, a lean and leathered legendary figure known in every port from South Street in New York to Maine. Zeb was a true American folk hero, famous for his wit, abnormal strength, and seamanship; it was said he could sail to Chicago in a heavy dew.

VACATIONER, MENEMSHA, 1973

*"Can't tell you how much I am looking forward to go to the island,"
Eisie wrote after a grueling schedule photographing in Brazil, Bermuda, and the Bahamas. "Since about three days am trying to put
slides together for island show" (the yearly program that was given for
the Old Sculpin Art Gallery at the Old Whaling Church).*

*He arrived the first of August and in no time was walking the
beaches and down at Menemsha greeting old friends, where he saw
this vacationer sitting on the jetty and used his telephoto lens to take
the picture.*

ARTISTS AT WORK, MENEMSHA

Menemsha has always been popular with artists as well as writers and other intellectuals.

Gay Head Cliffs, which has been a major scenic attraction since the nineteenth century. Although fishing and farming continue, the resort business dominates every aspect of the island's economy today.

Eisie was so taken with the island that after returning to New York, he came back to the Vineyard for two weeks of vacation. He continued to return each summer, and increasingly he found the rural up-island areas the most interesting. In the summer of 1950, he and his wife, Kathy, stayed at Menemsha Inn, where he has spent every vacation since that time.

Whether he was taking a picture of an antique rocking chair on an empty Oak Bluffs porch, a regatta in Edgartown, or Menemsha in the moonlight, Eisie has enjoyed his summers spent on the Vineyard. For nearly half a century, he has been a familiar figure walking along the windswept beaches of Gay Head and Chilmark, wearing his porkpie hat and carrying two cameras, one with black-and-white film and one with color. He loves photographing nature here—moving silently and quickly, as unobtrusive as the early morning mist rising

THORNTON WILDER, EDGARTOWN, 1975

"He was a wonderful man and very easy to photograph," Eisie remembers of the time he drove to Thornton Wilder's cottage near South Beach.

Wilder first came to the island in 1960, and later his sister, with whom he lived, bought the summer cottage. A brilliant playwright and author, he won the Pulitzer Prize three times: for The Bridge of San Luis Rey, The Skin of Our Teeth, and Our Town. His play The Matchmaker became the hit musical comedy Hello, Dolly!

Wilder was sympathetic to young people, particularly in the turbulent 1960s and early 1970s, and noted in a Vineyard Gazette interview, "If you haven't got a lot of protest in you when you're young, you can't hope to be a useful conservative when you are old" (December 12, 1975).

He usually worked while he was on the island and wrote his final novel, Theophilus North, here. Wilder died unexpectedly six months after Eisie took this photograph.

SOMERSET MAUGHAM, GAY HEAD, 1944

Somerset Maugham spent the summers of 1940–1944 at the Colonial Inn in Edgartown, where he was able to accomplish a lot of work in the mornings and enjoy socializing in the afternoons and evenings. An avid bridge player, he also liked to swim in the ocean and walk the beaches, where he is shown here in the summer of 1944. He was constantly invited to parties. The actress Katharine Cornell, who spent her summers on the island and acted in Maugham's play The Constant Wife, met him for the first time at a clambake here.

Maugham became quite fond of Mr. and Mrs. Thomas Chirgwin, the owners of the inn, and they arranged to have breakfast served to him in bed, as was his custom. In the early summer of 1943, the secretary who always accompanied him became ill, and he had to leave the island. Mr. Chirgwin's wife, Katherine, agreed to type his manuscript of The Razor's Edge. She remembers, "He wrote in longhand and didn't cross his t's or dot his i's, so it took me quite awhile to catch on. He was a lovely man. . . . It was a joy to have him at the inn."

LILLIAN HELLMAN, VINEYARD HAVEN, 1975

The late Lillian Hellman was working on her book Scoundrel Time *when Eisie photographed her on the lawn of her house overlooking Vineyard Haven Harbor. "It was water, not writing, that drew me here," she recalled of her first visits to the island in the 1940s* (Vineyard Gazette, *July 1984). In the 1950s, she and Dashiell Hammett bought their own house. Hellman kept a boat in Vineyard Haven Harbor, for the fine fishing in the waters around the island was one of the diversions from work she loved. Noted author John Hersey was also an avid fisherman, and these two friends often went out together for bluefish.*

A successful but controversial person, Hellman worked constantly and wrote Toys in the Attic *and parts of her books and plays, including* The Children's Hour, The Little Foxes, An Unfinished Woman, *and* Pentimento, *while on the island.*

RUTH GORDON, EDGARTOWN, 1975

For over twenty years, Academy Award-winning actress and writer Ruth Gordon and her husband, author/playwright Garson Kanin, spent summers in their house in Edgartown. They worked in separate offices in the house but took time to have tea or dine with friends. Thornton Wilder was a close friend, and Ruth was a member of the cast of his play The Matchmaker.

For relaxation she loved to walk. Well into her eighties, this diminutive figure would be seen walking at sunrise along the roadside at Chappaquiddick or down to the lighthouse, where she might meet Henry Hough. In the evenings, Ruth and Garson would often stroll around town, stopping to chat or admire a garden.

Ruth Gordon's books, interviews, and lectures all touted the importance of staying busy and young at heart. In her eighty-eighth year, she agreed to introduce her film Harold and Maude *at a special showing to raise money for the Old Sculpin Art Gallery. Two weeks later, she died in her sleep at the place she had always called home.*

GAY HEAD LIGHTHOUSE AND KEEPER'S HOUSE, 1937

This photograph shows the famous Fresnel lens (installed in 1856) before it was moved to the grounds of the Dukes County Historical Society. Augustin-Jean Fresnel of France developed this type of lens, which was assembled with compound lenses instead of the mirrors formerly used in lighthouses and searchlights. When the Fresnel lens was replaced by an automated one, the keeper's house was torn down.

off a Chilmark pond as he catches a sunning seal or waits for some sea gulls to give him the composition he would like or for the proper light to photograph his beloved cosmos.

Eisie's enthusiasm for the area has been the stimulus for his concern for its welfare. For over twenty years, he has given slide lectures to help raise money for the Old Sculpin Art Gallery for its maintenance and for art programs on the island. He has also acted on his interest in the preservation of the fragile environment of the island, which has been extensively damaged by man's thoughtless actions in the past. His affection for the Vineyard has remained deep through the years.

So here it is—Eisie's long love affair with Martha's Vineyard.

SUNSET AT MENEMSHA, 1967

"*The sunsets at Menemsha are breathtaking, and I took many, many photographs. It's like the ocean; every one is always different, and every wave is always different. The light, the colors are so beautiful—I never get tired of them.*" In a recent discussion, Eisie agreed that this photograph is reminiscent of the Luminist work of the Hudson River School of artists, notably that of Frederic Church.

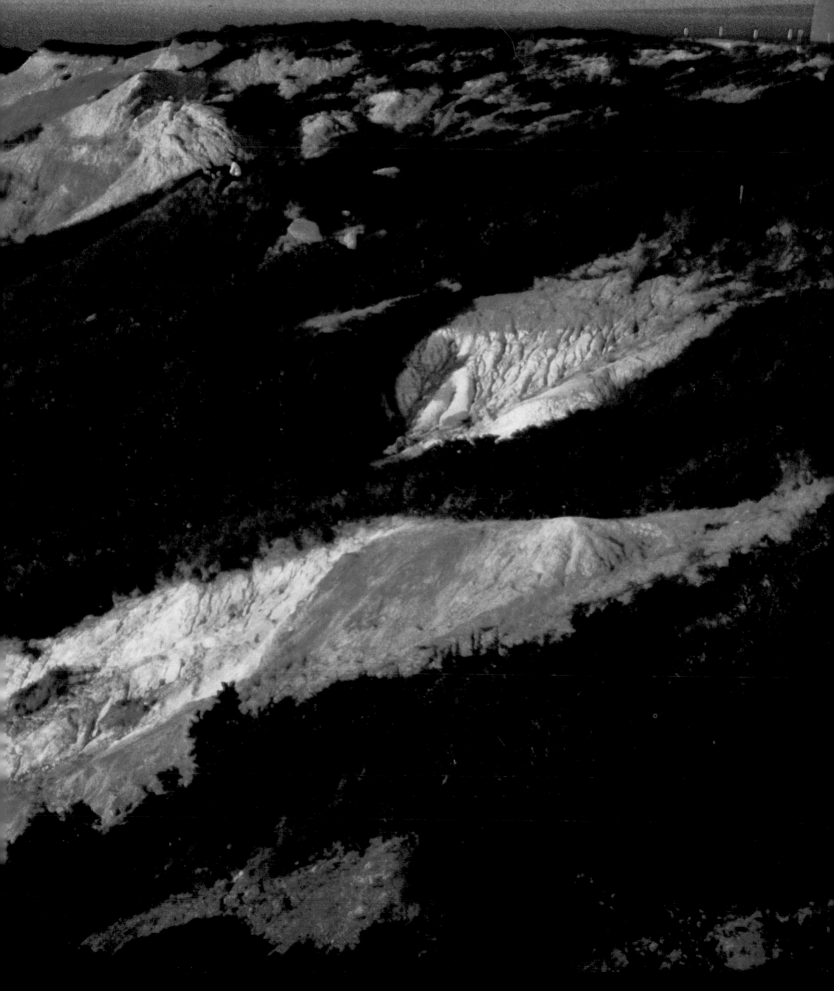

GAY HEAD

GAY HEAD

CLIFFS AT SUNSET, 1969

(Preceding overleaf) *The twisted strata of these multicolored cliffs tell the history of millions of years of the earth's formation and are of particular interest to geologists and paleontologists. Fossils of camels, whales, and elephants have been found in the clay. In the past, the cliffs were a source of income for the Gay Head Indians, who dug the clay out by hand and shipped it to mainland potteries on coastal schooners.*

British sailors named Gay Head in the seventeenth century, and reference to the cliffs is found in ships' logs and journals. They were a landmark to sailors outward bound on voyages that sometimes lasted years, and for those whaleships returning to New Bedford or the Vineyard, the cliffs were the first sight of home.

The colors were breathtaking in the 1960s, but now most of the red clay is gone. However, the cliffs remain the island's premier attraction, as they have been for over a century.

GAY HEAD CLIFFS

For the artist and the photographer, it is an endless challenge to capture the color and rhythms of the cliffs. The setting envelopes the senses: the colors in the cliffs themselves, the sapphire blue of the sea with fluffs of white marking the shoals offshore, the dull roar and rumble of the waves tumbling ashore, the smell of salt in the prevailing southwest winds, and those brilliant sunsets as the sun slips below the horizon—always changing, always stunning.

SEAL SUNNING, 1966

Although migrating seals are often spotted around the island in the winter, it is unusual to see them in the summer months. Eisie waited patiently for the perfect pose, and this seal was most accommodating.

EROSION OF CLIFFS, 1962

Most of the red clay shown here has now either fallen into the sea or been covered with vegetation. While there has been a great deal of erosion, through the years tourists have done extensive damage, and today it is against the law to climb on them.

One day Eisie saw two boys digging into the red clay, and he was furious. At that time there were no restrictions, but he shouted at the children to stop.

"They are just having fun," the parents protested. Eisie answered, "It took nature millions of years to create this. They should leave it alone. Tell them to stop it."

SAILBOAT NEAR GAY HEAD, 1971

"It was a gorgeous August afternoon, and I was planning to photograph just the cliffs when I spotted two sailboats over near Cuttyhunk Island across Vineyard Sound. I thought, if I wait, maybe I'll get something. Several hours passed before I was able to get this photograph. I used a Leicaflex set on a tripod and a 400-mm lens.

"When the sailboat finally came into view, a father and his son, who had a camera, were standing behind me. The father said to the boy, 'Mr. Eisenstaedt would like that scene.' I turned and said, 'I am Mr. Eisenstaedt.' He got very angry and stalked off."

GAY HEAD CLIFFS

(This page and right) Each summer when Eisie returns to the island for the month of August, he goes out on the beaches and cliffs to observe the changes that have taken place the preceding winter. The outcrop of clay at right managed to survive several years.

HONEYMOON COUPLE AT GAY HEAD, 1946
*In the summer of 1946, as World War II was ending, Eisie stayed at
the Totem Pole Inn in Gay Head. "There was still no electricity in
Gay Head in those days. I spotted this honeymoon couple standing by
a cottage one afternoon and used my Linhof camera, 4 x 5."*

FREIGHTER AGROUND, 1948

"I happened to be on the cliffs when I saw this freighter aground on Devil's Bridge. But I wouldn't have taken this photograph without the clouds." Eisie is noted for his unique compositions using cloud formations.

GAY HEAD LIGHTHOUSE, 1967

The Gay Head Lighthouse guards the western entrance to Vineyard Sound. Its flashing light warns ships off Devil's Bridge, a great reef of glacial boulders extending out from the cliffs.

The original manned lighthouse here, built in 1799, was one of the first revolving lights in the country. The wooden works often became swollen in the damp weather, and then the keeper or his wife had to spend the night turning the light by hand. In 1856, a larger steel structure was installed containing the famous Fresnel lens constructed from over a thousand crown glass prisms. That light was replaced by the present automated one in 1952. The Fresnel light is now housed on the Dukes County Historical Society grounds in a replica of the original watch room, and it is lit every evening in the summer.

INDIAN BAPTIST CHURCH, 1948

In a setting of rolling fields edged with magnificent stone walls high above the Atlantic Ocean stands the Gay Head Indian Baptist Church, the front facing seaward. It dates to the seventeenth century and is the oldest Indian Baptist church in North America.

"When I photograph people, I always look at the background first, but not so with landscapes, as you can see here. The foreground is what I look at first, and it's very important."

ZACK'S CLIFFS

"This scene with those beautiful dunes in the background reminded me of tiny Christmas trees growing in the sand, and the light was perfect."

DUSTY MILLER

Zack's Cliffs are on the eastern end of the Gay Head beach, and over the years Eisie has walked miles there, stopping to photograph what appealed to him. The dusty miller plant is found on the beaches and dunes all over the island.

It is believed Zack's Cliffs were named for Zachary Howwosee, the last preacher of the Church of the Standing Order, which was recognized in the 1700s as orthodox in Massachusetts. He was the last person to address his congregation in the Wampanoag language.

MR. AND MRS. DAVID VANDERHOOP, 1952

The late Mr. and Mrs. David Vanderhoop in their Gay Head home in the summer of 1952, where Eisie found Mr. Vanderhoop at work on a painting. A fisherman most of his life, David had also served in the Coast Guard and worked on the island's freight boat, the Eben A. Thatcher. *But it was his interest in art, which began when he bought his first paints at a very young age for $1.05, that was his lifetime passion, and he developed into an accomplished artist. Self-taught, he became known for his seascapes and landscapes. At the urging of friends, he had his first public show when he was seventy years old; he was often compared to Grandma Moses for that reason.*

MR. AND MRS. NAPOLEON BONAPARTE MADISON, AUGUST 1969

Napoleon Bonaparte Madison, medicine man of the Pokanocket Confederacy (also called the Wampanoag Indian tribe), and his wife, Nanetta. Admired and respected by all who knew him, Napoleon went to sea on whaleships as a young man, serving as both boatsteerer and deckhand. He was also a farmer and craftsman. The bead necklaces and bracelets he made were sold in his wife's gift shop, now run by his son, Luther. Involved in community affairs all his life, Napoleon was the impetus for the creation of the town library.

The Gay Headers were so well known as able and courageous seamen that it was considered good luck to have them aboard a whaleship. They were in great demand as boatsteerer, the man who would stand in the bow of the longboat and cast the first harpoon in the whale. The only Vineyarder to harpoon a white whale was a Gay Head Indian and a friend of Napoleon's, Amos Smalley. These Gay Headers were immortalized in Herman Melville's great classic, Moby-Dick.

BERTHA VANDERHOOP GILES, JULY 1937

His first summer on the island, Eisie found Bertha Vanderhoop Giles, a member of a distinguished Gay Head family, climbing up the cliffs with a bucket of the clay she used to make pots to sell to summer tourists. Bertha was eighteen years old at the time and explained to Eisie that this was a way members of her family made enough money to acquire a college education. She would set the pots out in the sun to dry, then finish and polish them and take them to her gift shop on the cliffs.

Excursion boats would bring tourists from the mainland and the eastern end of the island to a pier near the base of the cliffs. They would then be taken up the cliffs by oxcart to picnic, purchase the Indian crafts, and admire the Fresnel lighthouse lens along with the view. It was a popular activity from the 1880s through the turn of the century, but when automobile transportation became more common and travel about the island easier, the excursion trips ceased and the pier was swallowed up by the sea. Bertha and other Gay Headers, however, continued to make and sell their crafts.

CHILMARK

CHILMARK

SAILBOAT RACES, 1968

There are no yacht clubs on the western end of Martha's Vineyard, but that doesn't deter sailors from racing there. Any boat twenty feet or under can participate in the weekly races on Menemsha Pond, and many join the fray. The expertise of some skippers is no match for their extraordinary accomplishments elsewhere, but they all approach the race with competitive zeal, determined to win in their Sunfish, Sailfish, catboat, or sloop. Dr. Jerome Wiesner, former president of M.I.T., and Nobel Prize-winners Robert M. Solow and Franco Modigliani are out to do battle along with others from the arts and academic world.

HERRING CREEK, 1968

(Preceding overleaf) For over two centuries, herring (also known as alewives) were an important part of the islander's diet and economy. They were eaten fresh or cured and also exported. The Indians taught the early settlers how to catch herring in weirs when the fish were running up the creeks in the early spring to spawn.

This notable creek, which marks the town line between Gay Head and Chilmark, meanders from Menemsha Pond to Squibnocket Pond. It borders the former home of the late Thomas Hart Benton on Menemsha Pond.

JACKSON POLLOCK, CHILMARK, 1937

Pollock was a student of Benton's at the Arts Students League in New York City and a favorite of the family. Shown above seated on the right, he visited the Bentons often from 1931 to 1937, living in the chicken coop they called "Jack's Shack." He baby-sat for their son "TP" (shown here patting the dog) and helped Tom around the place by clearing brush, chopping wood, and gardening. They were relaxed, peaceful times for the struggling young artist who went on to lead such a turbulent life.

While they had sharply divergent views about art, still Benton and his young protégé respected one another. "Pollock was a damn fine artist. His work I like very much, but the meanings behind it I would question—he left out the human element," Benton observed in Thomas Hart Benton: A Portrait *by Polly Burroughs.*

When asked about Benton in a New Yorker magazine article in 1950, Pollock remarked that he was "damn grateful to Tom. He drove his kind of realism at me so hard I bounced right into nonobjective painting."

THOMAS HART BENTON, 1969

Thomas Hart Benton first came to Martha's Vineyard in July 1920. For twenty-five dollars, Benton and two friends rented a small shingled barn for the summer. There was a closet-size space for a kerosene stove, no electricity or running water was available, and they slept in a hay loft. The setting afforded a striking view of the Atlantic Ocean and Vineyard Sound. For Benton, born and raised in Missouri and struggling to establish himself in New York, the change was as startling as it was to be for Eisie seventeen years later. It became a way of life for Benton and his wife, Rita, and they continued to spend summers here until he died in 1975.

Here on the island Benton felt "you got in touch with what was real." In the summer of 1922, Benton turned his back on modern art, which he had come to abhor, and painted his first Regionalist portrait, which was of the deaf-mute farmers George and Sabrina West. It was the start of the Regionalist work for which he became famous.

STONE WALLS, 1969

Stone walls tell the history of an area and lend as much character to the island as the fishermen's boathouses at Menemsha. Framing a field and snaking over the moors and meadows to reach down to the shore and ponds, they discipline the contours and boundaries while confining sheep and cattle.

This huge wall created its own design, forming peepholes that provided Eisie with a unique opportunity to photograph some boats on Chilmark's Quitsa Pond.

CANOE, CHILMARK, 1960

Alongside a Chilmark pond, a canoe lies waiting for its owner. There are freshwater ponds all over the island providing quiet backwaters to explore.

NASHAQUITSA POND, CHILMARK, 1977

Called Quitsa Pond for short, this setting is typical of many areas where green ribbons of marsh grass fringe the ponds, mallow and other wildflowers bloom, and cattails flourish in the brackish waters.

NASHAQUITSA POND, FEBRUARY 1952

The rhythms of the season and the sea are woven into the very fabric of island life, and winters, up-island in particular, are quiet times. Many houses are closed for the season; raw, bone-chilling winds sweep across the deserted beaches and dunes; and a light dusting of snow outlines the island's contours, framed by the grey green sea. Lush plants edging the tidal ponds and bays in summer are frozen hummocks in winter covered with a marshmallow coating of ice and snow. Nashaquitsa Pond here is partially frozen, and scallopers' boats lie idle on the shore.

BOATHOUSE, QUITSA POND

CHILMARK CLIFFS
Wind and wave have sculpted the cliffs for centuries, and more shoreline is lost to the sea each year. These eroding cliffs soaring one hundred feet or more above the ocean are on Roger Baldwin Beach. A prominent member of an intellectual group that began summering in Chilmark and Gay Head in the 1930s, Baldwin was one of the founders of the American Civil Liberties Union. For many years he owned a large tract of beachfront land along the south shore.

SQUIBNOCKET BEACH, 1970

A stormy day in August with an angry sea sweeping the beaches and battering the dunes. It is estimated that three feet of shore a year are washed into the Atlantic Ocean. Frequently houses have to be moved back as the erosion eats away the cliffs and dunes.

LUCY VINCENT BEACH

A stretch of beach that is similar to many areas along the south side of the island. It is open to residents and guests of Chilmark only. Eisie's sister-in-law, Lucille Kaye, is in the foreground.

ROCK ON SOUTH BEACH, 1974

Walking along Lucy Vincent Beach towards Gay Head, Eisie found
this huge stone. "For ten years I photographed this stone on different
days—sometimes cloudy, sometimes in bright sun. It fascinated me."

LUCY VINCENT BEACH, 1977

"*I was standing on a cliff at the Lucy Vincent Beach in Chilmark photographing cloud formations when I saw this girl come running along the edge of the surf with her dog. So often it is the unexpected that provides the opportunity for an unusual picture. I had a 200-mm lens with me and had time to attach it, using a light yellow filter with a 1/1000-second exposure to freeze motion.*"

BLACK CLAY, SOUTH BEACH

The black, white, and red clays found on the cliffs in Chilmark and Gay Head present Eisie with a new sculpture each year. "*This was so beautiful. I went back the next summer, but it was all gone—swept out to sea.*"

HUGE STONE, 1979

Tremendous boulders remain on the beach, but Eisie usually finds the background changed from year to year.

GOLDENROD, 1965

A fishing and farming community for nearly three centuries, Chilmark is a town of hills with undulating grey stone walls extending to the sea. Trees are sculpted close to the ground by relentless winds, and the rhythmic roar of the sea is heard far inland. The wildflowers begin painting the fields, roadsides, and marshes with their colorful palettes in June. Bright yellow Scotch broom is followed by white daisies, rugosa rose, beach pea, black-eyed Susans, Queen Anne's lace, chicory, orange butterfly weed, roses, thistles, purple asters, and seventeen species of goldenrod.

BERRIES, 1968

In earlier times, people could eat for almost nothing in the summer. There were fish, clams to be dug, one's own vegetable garden, and a bountiful supply of fruit: strawberries, raspberries, thimbleberries, grapes, beach plums, and blackberries that ripen in late summer when the goldenrod is in bloom. Eisie found these alongside an old stone wall in Chilmark; he kept the background out of focus to emphasize the colors of the ripening berries.

KEITH'S FARM, 1969

*The barn at Keith's farm in Chilmark, with its stone wall and
split-rail fence, is like many on the island.*

RED COSMOS, BEETLEBUNG CORNER, 1972

"*I have always had a passion for cosmos—they're so graceful—and I've photographed them many times with all kinds of lenses, filters, and prisms.*" They are also a favorite of Vineyarders and can be found in gardens all over the island.

DORY IN MARSH, 1965

An old wooden dory lying in the marsh was a familiar sight in the past, but not so common today. This appeared in Life Magazine.

BOY CRABBING, 1969
The still water casts a perfect reflection of a young boy looking for crabs or bait.

HILLSIDE, 1980
"I used my Nikon with a 35-mm PC lens and attached a polarizing filter." This was taken on the road leading down to Menemsha. Just as others do all over the island, this tree bends to the will of the prevailing southwest winds.

MENEMSHA

MENEMSHA HARBOR, 1937

In 1937, Menemsha was a fishing port filled with workboats. There was no marina or Coast Guard boat building. The basin is filled with catboats and larger fishing boats, and a lone fisherman rows his wooden dory through the harbor.

Before the turn of the century, Menemsha was known as Creekville and was just a narrow waterway leading from Vineyard Sound into Menemsha Pond, with shifting sands and currents precluding easy access. The fishing industry was located at Lobsterville across the harbor. In 1905, the opening into Menemsha Pond from the sea was dredged and a stone jetty and causeway erected to enclose the west side of the basin. It was an active fishing port called Menemsha by 1910; the name probably comes from an Indian word meaning "still water."

Rebuilding after the hurricane wiped out Menemsha in 1938 included putting in the present bulkhead. Dutcher Dock, along the east side of the basin, is named for Rodney Dutcher, a Vineyard native who became a well-known Washington journalist.

Today there are many pleasure boats in the harbor, but it is the fishing boats and fishermen's boathouses that give Menemsha its charm and unpretentious character, its indigenous relationship with the sea that has gone on for over three centuries.

HARBOR AND QUEEN ANNE'S LACE, 1962
*Queen Anne's lace provides the foreground for this shot of Menemsha
Harbor looking seaward on a summer morning.*

CALM MORNING, 1956

"I could never take this picture again on an August day. It's too crowded now." The nearly empty harbor of Menemsha on a morning in the 1950s afforded a beautiful view the length of the harbor when the water was flat calm.

FRED LITTLETON, HARBORMASTER, 1984

A longtime summer resident of Chilmark, Fred Littleton decided to give up his law practice in Wayne, Pennsylvania, and move to the island. He became Menemsha Harbormaster and now devotes his time to two lifelong interests: boatbuilding and sailing.

MENEMSHA HARBOR, MAY 1937

The south end of Menemsha's boat basin in 1937, when there were few summer people in the area and it was primarily a fishing port.

BUOY, MENEMSHA, 1981
A huge buoy at Menemsha across from Dutcher's Dock.

LOBSTER POTS ON DUTCHER DOCK, 1974
Lobster pots and their buoys piled up in late summer on Dutcher Dock, where they will be cleaned and painted for another season.

CALM HARBOR IN SUMMER, 1969
Menemsha Harbor in late summer with both fishing boats and pleasure boats tied up at the piers.

RUSTING ANCHOR, MENEMSHA, 1953
"I see things other people don't see," Eisie has said, and this setting with an antique car in the background was certainly something few people would notice.

ANCHOR CHAIN
The color and twisted shape of this rusting anchor chain on the dock at
Menemsha appealed to Eisie.

ROCKY SHORE, 1963
A section of rocky shore with seaweed and barnacle-encrusted rocks.

MENEMSHA HARBOR, AUGUST 1971
A summer scene in Menemsha in the early 1970s framed by nets used on the draggers.

UNITED STATES COAST GUARD STATION
The United States Coast Guard Station is on a bluff above Menemsha Harbor; the boat building is down on the harbor. They respond to all emergencies around the island and in the general area.

DOCKS IN FOG, 1968

Often thick fog rolls in from offshore cloaking Menemsha Harbor in cotton batting, and boats stay in port waiting for better weather. The quiet stillness is broken by the mournful moan of a foghorn droning on in the distance, and the smell of low tide fills the air. "Even the sea gull sounded soggy! I used my Nikon with 105-mm lens."

HARBOR ON FOGGY MORNING, 1967

*Fishing and other boats are tied up in Menemsha Harbor on a foggy
morning.*

HURRICANE CAROL, AUGUST 1954

Labor Day weekend was coming up, and the harbors and hotels were filled with vacationers having one last fling. There had been warnings of a hurricane in the South Atlantic, but at 6 A.M., one radio station reported Hurricane Carol was veering out to sea and would not hit the New England coast. There were other conflicting reports, and at 6:30 A.M., the bulletins were changed: The storm would hit the area between 11 A.M. and 3 P.M., but the winds would only be about 60 miles per hour with occasional gusts to 90 mph.

By 9:30 A.M. the storm had hit, the tide was rising, and wind-driven seas began to batter the island as the storm peaked. The dreaded flood tide and 94-mph winds wiped out Menemsha, cut off Gay Head, and left Vineyard Haven waterfront a pile of lumber. The raging waves dumped boats in the middle of fields, carried boathouses out to sea, and smashed yachts, schooners, and powerboats to bits.

Eisie and Kathy were staying at the Menemsha Inn, and Eisie could hardly wait to get out and photograph. As soon as the storm had subsided in early afternoon, he hurried on down to the waterfront.

"I dressed in my bathing suit with my Leica camera in a plastic bag under my oil slicker and walked on down to the harbor. There was still plenty of wind and rain. Tom Benton was there painting this tragic scene. I would take out my camera, snap quickly, then put it under my slicker. When it calmed down, the light and color were fantastic."

HURRICANE CAROL, AUGUST 1954

HURRICANE CAROL, AUGUST 1954

(This page and right) The destruction on Dutcher Dock after Hurricane Carol. Captain Donald Poole's *fishing boat, the* Dorothy & Everett, *and a catboat were smashed against the dock and heavily damaged.*

HURRICANE CAROL, AUGUST 1954

The calm after the storm shows Stuart Knight's boathouse, decorated with swordfish tails, floating in the middle of Menemsha Harbor.

HURRICANE EDNA, SEPTEMBER 1954

Ten days later there was another ominous warning—Hurricane Edna was heading towards the New England coast and might hit the island. As the evening wore on and the wind and seas mounted, stores ran out of candles, kerosene, flashlights, and some food staples. Everyone "battened down the hatches" and waited, hoping the island would be spared. Eisie and Kathy were still at the Menemsha Inn, so he decided to put on a slide show as long as the electricity held. His colored slides of the famous rain forests of Surinam and of the Duke of Edinburgh's recent trip to Canada delighted the audience and momentarily took everyone's mind off the roaring winds, flying branches, and stinging salt spray.

"The wind gusted to 110 miles per hour, worse than Carol," Everett Poole explained, "but it came at low tide and we had already been wiped out. The damage had been done, so Edna caused fewer problems."

MENEMSHA BIGHT, 1967
A *fleet of sailboats racing just off Menemsha Harbor at Menemsha
Bight, known for years as an excellent fishing spot.*

CAPTAIN DONALD POOLE, 1971

*"He was a prominent man in Menemsha, and I photographed him
many times, usually in his boathouse on the dock in Menemsha."* The
contents of Captain Poole's boathouse reflect the history of the seaport,
and Eisie generally found him sitting in his captain's chair surrounded by reminders of a lifetime at sea. A fisherman and later in life
a lobsterman, Captain Poole was from an old island family whose
roots run deep in Vineyard lore. He was a recognized authority on
whaling and often consulted by historians. Poole's Fish Market, run
by his son Everett, has been a Menemsha landmark for years.

SAILING AT SUNSET, 1956
A small sailing dinghy ghosts along in Menemsha Harbor at sunset.

DAY AT THE BEACH, 1976
(Preceding overleaf) *Menemsha's public beach, which runs along the
north shore adjacent to the entrance to the harbor.*

REFLECTION IN BOATHOUSE WINDOW

BOYS DIVING, 1964

DUSK IN MENEMSHA, 1962

In late afternoon, the wind usually drops, the harbor and water are quiet, and the sunsets at Menemsha are spectacular. This photograph was included in an exhibition of Eisie's work at the Time & Life Building in Rockefeller Center.

Eisie remembers that at the opening reception, a man and his wife who apparently had visited Cape Cod recently were looking at this, and Eisie's wife, Kathy, overheard the woman speaking to her husband in an angry voice. "I told you we should have taken that ferry to Martha's Vineyard," she snapped at her husband.

JETTY AT NIGHTFALL, 1967
A cruising boat anchored for the night just beyond the jetty at the entrance to Menemsha Harbor.

THE TEXAS TOWER
"On a clear night from the lawn of the Menemsha Inn you can see the Texas Tower, which is at the entrance to Buzzards Bay. Everything has to be exactly right, and I was only able to get this photograph two times in thirty-five years. No wind, no clouds—it has to be absolutely still. This was taken with a Nikon camera and a telephoto lens."

The tower, named for its similarity to a Texas oil rig, is a navigational guide for ships and replaced a lightship that had been there for years.

QUEEN ANNE'S LACE

"This was taken at Menemsha, but you can't do it anymore. It's too crowded and the flowers get trampled, and there are more buildings there. I used a Leica camera to which was attached a Visoflex housing plus a 400-mm lens and a very light red filter. This was taken from a low angle on a tripod."

MOONLIT HARBOR, SEPTEMBER 1963

A harvest moon casts its glow across Menemsha Harbor and the fishing fleet in early fall.

WEST TISBURY

WEST TISBURY

WEST TISBURY FARM, 1983
(Preceding overleaf) *A farm in West Tisbury with cedar trees and some goldenrod in the foreground.*

BIRD-WATCHERS, 1969
The island is a bird-watcher's paradise, and guided tours are scheduled all year. In both the spring and fall, migrating birds touch down to rest and feed. A large number are indigenous to the island year-round, but there are also Arctic birds who settle in the winter and those that come north for the summer months, like the tourists.

SWANS, OLD MILL POND, 1960
Feeding the ducks and swans at the Old Mill Pond in West Tisbury is a favorite activity in the summer. The mill across the road is now headquarters for the Martha's Vineyard Garden Club. Originally it was a factory for the manufacture of satinet, a heavy wool fabric woven from sheep's wool for seamen's pea jackets.

FISHER'S FARM, LONG COVE, 1971

(**This page and right**) *For two centuries, fishing and farming were the primary means of livelihood on the Vineyard. It was not unusual to see farms alongshore, where sheep and cattle grazed by coves and inlets and a fishing dory lay alongside a hay rake or a plough. Sheep raising was prevalent in the eighteenth and nineteenth centuries.*

Fisher's farm at Long Cove in West Tisbury is a reminder of earlier times, with cattle and freshly sheared sheep feeding together on a beautiful August afternoon.

When Eisie was taking these photographs, a bull emerged from nowhere. Eisie, who was accompanied by friends, took immediate command, as he had had the same experience at a ranch in Texas. He ordered his companions to stop dead, then walk slowly to safety.

SUNFLOWERS, 1968

"Sometimes I look with telephoto eyes and sometimes with wide-angle eyes." Here Eisie found one of those magnificent stone walls and some large sunflowers casting their yellow glow. A favorite flower of islanders for centuries, they are planted beside barns and in gardens.

JOSHUA SLOCUM'S HOUSE, 1968

With its sag back roof and overhang, this unique example of an early-eighteenth-century house was home to an equally unusual sailor at the turn of the century. In 1898, after returning from his famous solo voyage around the world in his thirty-seven-foot sloop, Captain Joshua Slocum decided to settle down on the island. He chose the Vineyard, he said, after reading the dates on the tombstones—he anticipated having a long and leisurely old age.

Here Slocum wrote his classic, Sailing Alone Around the World, and did some lecturing and farming. But he became restless and the lure of the sea obsessed him; so once again he set out on another voyage, departing the island in 1909. He was never heard from again.

MR. AND MRS. ALBERT LITTLEFIELD, 1976

Each summer Eisie would visit the Littlefields, and one afternoon Eisie remarked on the clothes and fancy hats that Peg Littlefield put on her scarecrows. "Do you have any old clothes in the attic you could put on? I'd like to photograph you dressed up that way."

They were delighted with the idea. Al comes from an old Vineyard family, and they have one of those New England attics that are usually a treasure trove of family memorabilia.

SCARECROW, WEST TISBURY

Although Eisie drives carefully, he screeched to a halt when he spotted some handsomely dressed scarecrows protecting a large vegetable field. He went up to the charming grey farmhouse, introduced himself to Peg and Al Littlefield, and said he would like to wander about and photograph them. This introduction, via the scarecrows, was the beginning of a wonderful friendship.

AGRICULTURAL FAIR

(This page, 1969, and left, 1984) Eisie has always gone to the agricultural fair held each August in West Tisbury and photographed, his favorite subject being one of the oldest and most crowd-pleasing events, the horse-drawing contest. He is taken with these huge dray horses and their draymen, with whips flashing, shouting at the horses to move ahead. "These are difficult photographs to do to get the right angle. For years I photographed these huge, powerful animals straining to pull those heavy loads."

CARNIVAL RIDES, AGRICULTURAL FAIR

(This page, 1974, and right, 1973) Over a century old, the West Tisbury agricultural fair was originally held in the fall after crops were in, root cellars filled for the winter, and the farmers had time to exhibit their late crops and livestock. As the island became more of a summer resort, the date was changed to August, and a Ferris wheel, merry-go-round, and other attractions have been added. Eisie used his Nikon camera for these double exposures.

BIKING TO WEST TISBURY

Biking is a widespread activity on the Vineyard. This group is traveling along the South Road to West Tisbury from Edgartown. Many hardy visitors like to tour the island from Edgartown through West Tisbury and the hilly Chilmark and Gay Head area and back to Edgartown via the north side of the island.

HORSEBACK RIDING

A group from a riding academy in West Tisbury, where horseback riding has become a popular sport in recent years. The trails in some areas take riders along the beach as well as through woods and fields.

PARSONAGE POND, FEBRUARY 1952

When he was on the island in February 1952 doing a story for Life Magazine, Eisie found this group of children skating on the pond near the center of West Tisbury. There are many such ponds scattered about the island, but due to the proximity of the Gulf Stream offshore and rapid changes in the weather, the ice usually does not last long.

CONGREGATIONAL CHURCH

Herman Melville wrote in Moby-Dick ". . . pieces of wood in Nantucket are carried about like bits of the true cross in Rome . . . ," and so it was on the Vineyard, with wood so precious it was never thrown away. When a man moved from one town to another, he took his family, his livestock, and with the aid of oxen, his house.

Formerly beside the town cemetery, the Congregational church was moved to this site in the center of West Tisbury in 1865. It plays an important part in the town's activities, as lectures and musical programs are given there. The church stands on the corner of Music Street, which got its name a hundred years ago when every house on the street was reputed to have a piano.

KATHARINE GRAHAM, AUGUST 1987

Katharine Graham, publisher of the Washington Post, *is shown on the porch of Mohu, her summer place on a bluff on the north shore overlooking Vineyard Sound. Woods, marshland, ponds, and sea surround this quiet retreat, where she spends what time she can away from the demands of her business. Not only a brilliant businesswoman but also a renowned hostess, Katharine Graham has had Nancy Reagan, Henry Kissinger, and others prominent in government as her guests.*

INDIAN CEMETERY, 1969

Surrounded by ferns and wildflowers growing in the dappled shade, fieldstones mark an old Indian graveyard in Christiantown.

CHRISTIANTOWN, 1969

(This page and right) The history of Christiantown goes back to the first settlers. This ancient township in North Tisbury was started with a grant of one square mile given by Sachem Josias Keteanummin of Takemmy in 1659 as a new home for those Indians who, following the teachings of Governor Mayhew, had converted to Christianity.

The present meeting house, or chapel, in this lovely woodland setting was erected in 1829 to replace two earlier buildings. It has just six pews on either side of the center aisle and a tiny altar.

OAK BLUFFS
& TISBURY

TISBURY

TASHMOO SPRINGS, AUGUST 1987

(Preceding overleaf) Tashmoo Springs, which the Indians called Kehtashimet *("at the great spring"), was a source of drinking water for many years. Just outside of Vineyard Haven, it is surrounded by vibrant foliage and is adjacent to Lake Tashmoo, a large body of water opening into Vineyard Sound on the north side of the island.*

Eisie photographed his sister-in-law, Lucille Kaye, admiring the view and the pleasure boats riding at anchor in Lake Tashmoo.

WILLIAM STREET, VINEYARD HAVEN, AUGUST 1987

(Left and following overleaf) Unlike Edgartown, where many beautiful historic houses were built with whaling money, Vineyard Haven was primarily a port for all types of shipping traffic moving up and down the East Coast. Ships put into this busy seaport to replenish supplies, ride out a storm, or make repairs. Many Vineyarders were merchant seamen, master mariners with their own vessels, or pilots, and others ran successful businesses at the seaport. The most prosperous built these Greek Revival houses along William Street, now a historic district, in the mid-nineteenth century.

Captain Benjamin C. Cromwell's house (left) is Victorian and was built a bit later than the others on William Street, in 1873. He amassed his wealth as skipper of an old side-wheeler, Eagle Wings, *ferrying passssengers from New Bedford to Vineyard Haven. After the Civil War, when the resort boom in Oak Bluffs reached a feverish pitch, he bought a new ship, the* Monohansett.

MIKE WALLACE, VINEYARD HAVEN, 1975

"There is '60 Minutes,' and there is everything else," the New York Times *noted recently about this lucrative news program. Mike Wallace, one of the two original correspondents, has always been considered the backbone of the program and responsible for its initial success. To escape a grueling schedule, Mike comes to his summer home in Vineyard Haven for relaxation, and he usually plays tennis with Art Buchwald.*

Like other notables in television and the arts, Mike has graciously given programs to raise money for the Old Sculpin Art Gallery. The Old Whaling Church in Edgartown was filled to overflowing when Mike interviewed Thomas Hart Benton in a riveting, insightful program. Six months later, Benton was dead. And in the summer of 1984, Mike and Harry Reasoner put on a program called "What Make '60 Minutes' Tick?" Although the church holds five hundred people and the aisles were filled, four hundred more had to be turned away.

ART BUCHWALD, VINEYARD HAVEN, 1975

On the tennis court, Art Buchwald is known as a "lobber," according to his friend Mike Wallace, and he's as witty on the court as he is in print.

Buchwald has had a summer home in Vineyard Haven for a long time, and he has contributed his time and talent to raise money for the island's community services at their annual auction each summer. Dressed in a cowboy hat and chomping a cigar, he's the "Possible Dreams" auctioneer, offering such unique items as a sail with Walter Cronkite, lunch with Bill Styron, a tour of CBS with Mike Wallace, or a tour of the Washington Post *with Katharine Graham (where he guarantees you'll find out who "Deep Throat" really is!). His ad-libbing is excruciatingly funny, and he's the primary reason for the huge success of this annual fund-raiser.*

He is equally humorous in any setting. After spraining his ankle a few years ago playing tennis, Art became impatient waiting for it to heal and asked the local dry cleaner to wrap it in plastic so he could go swimming.

WILLIAM STYRON, AUGUST 1987

Highly acclaimed author William Styron and his family came to the island in 1959 and soon after purchased a lovely home overlooking Vineyard Haven Harbor, where they continue to spend long summer seasons. While his friends play tennis and sail, Styron, with the exception of a family game of croquet, works in a studio behind the house. He has a small writing desk in a studio with no clutter, and works in pencil, in longhand, on a yellow legal pad. He wrote much of his best-seller Sophie's Choice *here; among other honors, he received a Pulitzer Prize for* The Confessions of Nat Turner.

OAK BLUFFS

COTTAGES, OAK BLUFFS, 1972

The rise of the Methodist religion in the country was responsible for the initial development of Oak Bluffs, which was followed by an influx of summer vacationers in the latter part of the nineteenth century.

The settlement took root in 1835 when Oak Bluffs had its first Revivalist meeting in a grove of oak trees. Tents were placed in a circle around the podium, and this public forum for soul-searching brought increasingly larger crowds from the mainland each August. Revivalism swept the island as preachers gathered their flock of converts away from the Congregationalists, then the dominant sect. The fashionableness of camp meetings attracted the secular, and it became a preferred summer colony for both.

About the same time the tent owners decided to build little wooden houses on their tent sites at the campground, the inventions of the jigsaw and band saw dictated the architecture. By 1866, saws were buzzing night and day to meet the demand as these tiny cottages were built not ten feet apart in a circle around the imposing Tabernacle.

LADIES CHATTING, CAMPGROUND, 1937

His first summer on the island, Eisie found these ladies having a morning chat on the campground in Oak Bluffs. The house on the left, with fancy scrollwork and shingles like pigeon's feathers, is a good example of many houses here.

OAK BLUFFS, 1972

CAMPGROUND PORCHES

Each owner tried to outdo his neighbor with facades decorated with gables, turrets, scrollwork, balconies, cathedral windows, and fancily cut shingles, and they painted their lacy valentines in vivid rainbow hues. The rocking chairs were usually turned upside down at night so they wouldn't creak and to keep the dew off the chair seats. This Hansel-and-Gretel village is now a carefully preserved landmark of Carpenter Gothic architecture.

OAK BLUFFS, 1957

OAK BLUFFS, 1959

133

ILLUMINATION NIGHT, OAK BLUFFS, 1969

To celebrate the closing of the camp meeting every year, all the tents on the campground were lit with candles for Illumination Night. The tradition continued after the houses were electrified, and when a Japanese merchant in town began selling paper lanterns, everyone decorated their cottages with them for the event. Each August this miniature fairyland setting lights up like a Christmas tree.

Many musical programs and other events take place in the Tabernacle (above right) each summer. Now a national landmark, it was built in the center of the campground in 1879 to replace the original circus-style tent. Constructed of T irons, angle irons, and pipe, with wooden rafters supporting the corrugated roof, it is considered to be one of the largest wrought-iron structures in America.

TABERNACLE, 1969

CIRCUIT AVENUE, AUGUST 1937

A quiet moment on the main street in Oak Bluffs during Eisie's second visit to Martha's Vineyard. Today it is crowded with tourists all summer long.

MAIN STREET OF OAK BLUFFS, FEBRUARY 1952

"It was fascinating to see the island in the wintertime: no tourists, empty streets—beautiful." Here Eisie found only a lone bicycle rider and one car on Circuit Avenue and most shops closed and shuttered for winter.

OCEAN PARK, OAK BLUFFS, 1968

This lovely park faces the sea and is surrounded by large Carpenter Gothic houses generously covered with rococo designs similar to the ones of the tiny houses on the campground. They were constructed at the height of the building boom, when many vacationers came from cities in nearby Massachusetts and Rhode Island. A gazebo in the center is used for evening concerts under the stars.

BOY ON RAILING, OCEAN PARK

"That boy walking on the railing caught my eye. There's a really big drop on the other side. His sense of balance was amazing."

EDGARTOWN & CHAPPAQUIDDICK

EDGARTOWN

RACES, EDGARTOWN HARBOR, 1969

(Preceding overleaf) A busy Saturday afternoon in Edgartown Harbor as several boats wend their way to the outer harbor for the start of the weekly yacht club races. Five classes of sailboats race each week during the summer, and the annual Edgartown Regatta attracts participation by many yacht clubs in the southern New England area.

JAMES RESTON AND WALTER CRONKITE, 1975

America's favorite television journalist for years, Walter Cronkite is an ardent tennis player and yachtsman, who has chronicled his love of the sea in two well-received books: South By Southeast *and* North By Northeast. *Cronkite has been a summer resident of Edgartown for twenty years and keeps his beloved sailboat moored right off his waterfront summer house. Ray Ellis, a renowned artist and another island homeowner, illustrated the books with beautiful seascapes and landscapes of the coastal world he knows so well.*

Twenty-three years ago, the distinguished editor of the New York Times, *James Reston, bought the* Vineyard Gazette *from Henry Hough. The recipient of Pulitzer Prizes and many other honors, Reston spends some time on the island relaxing and on occasion challenges Walter to a fast game of tennis.*

BLACK PEARL, 1965

The topsail schooner Black Pearl *from Newport, Rhode Island, on a starboard tack sailing into Edgartown Harbor in a fine August sou'wester. The owner of the vessel at the time also owned the Black Pearl restaurant on the Newport waterfront, where he kept the vessel tied up. The schooner was a pleasure boat as well as used in the American Sail Training Programs.*

MAIN STREET, EDGARTOWN, JULY 1937

"*My first visit to Martha's Vineyard was an assignment for Life Magazine in July 1937. I had taken the train from New York City to New London, Connecticut, where I met Roy Larsen, publisher of Life. There had been a ferry strike, so he had come over from Nantucket, where he had a summer home, in his powerful speedboat, which had two engines. He dropped me off at the Edgartown Yacht Club pier, and I stayed for a week at what is now the Kelly house.*"

There were few stores in Edgartown in those days, and they supplied the small village with such essentials as hardware, food, and work clothes. Some summer gift and clothing stores closed for winter.

BOY ON A UNICYCLE, 1969

A side street in Edgartown. Familiar white picket fences frame these old houses nestled close together right on the street, which was the custom in early New England seacoast villages. Dahlias line the white fence on the left, and roses tumble over an arbor on the right. Roses thrive in Edgartown with the sea air and evening dew misting them, their sweet fragrance wafting out on the streets. They are found everywhere, their blossoms cascading over fences or gracing more formal gardens, where they are carefully pruned and often offset by beautiful English boxwoods.

DUKES COUNTY COURTHOUSE, EDGARTOWN, 1969

Built in 1858 to replace an earlier structure, the Dukes County Courthouse is one of the few brick buildings in the village. The county jail was also located here originally, and in 1860, a visiting journalist from the New York World *described the tiny jail as a "diminutive edifice constructed of massive blocks of boulder granite, whose appearance, size, and grated windows excited our surprise and merriment. . . . Constructed of four cells, two on a story, it could be readily set up, yard, fence, roof and all, in an ordinary-sized New York parlor." To add insult to injury with his patronizing remarks, the journalist concluded, "It adjoins a small wooden tenement, the dwelling of the deputy sheriff."*

The jail was torn down and a new one built on Upper Main Street in 1873. All the county's business is conducted here in the courthouse, including court sessions in the spring and fall.

METHODIST CHURCH, 1969

Known as the Old Whaling Church, this handsome Greek Revival building was erected at the time evangelical religion was sweeping the island. Captain John Morse, a whaleman, brought the lumber down from Maine. The handsome clock tower soars 92 feet and is visible to sailors far out at sea. Now belonging to the Martha's Vineyard Historical Preservation Society, it is the island's performing arts center where programs were held for the Old Sculpin Art Gallery and lectures and musical programs are currently given year-round. Church services are held in the summer months.

DOOR TO ST. ANDREW'S EPISCOPAL CHURCH

"It was the red door framed with that lovely shiny green ivy which caught my eye." Built in 1899, this small brick building has a pulpit made from the bow of an old fishing dory. Before that time, Episcopal services in Edgartown were held in a room over a dry goods store on Main Street.

DUKES COUNTY HISTORICAL SOCIETY, 1970
A model of a schooner in the window of one of the buildings of the island's major historical society. The buildings of Dukes County Historical Society are clustered in the center of Edgartown and filled with memorabilia from three centuries of island life.

ANTIQUE DRESSES, 1965
*(**Preceding overleaf**) The attic of the Cooke House on the Dukes County Historical Society grounds, with an attractive display of antique dresses. Built about 1765, the house is an exceptional example of a pre-revolutionary war building and was the office of Edgartown's customs collector in the early 1800s. Additional buildings on the grounds house a fine library, paintings, ship models, scrimshaw, log books, journals, and other interesting artifacts.*

TOMBSTONES FOR NANCY LUCE'S CHICKENS

"Passing a summer, several years since, at Edgartown . . . I became acquainted with a certain carver of tomb-stones . . . ," Nathaniel Hawthorne wrote in his essay "Chippings with a Chisel" from Twice-Told Tales. Hawthorne was staying at the Edgartown Inn when he came across Mr. Wigglesworth's marble shop down on the waterfront. The door was left open and people would wander in and out, watching the old man work away on his slabs of marble and granite while he discussed the requests from his customers. One unusual order came from a maiden lady in West Tisbury named Nancy Luce, who was so devoted to her chickens that she wrote poems about them to sell to summer tourists and had Wigglesworth carve tombstones for her favorite hens. Contemplating the tombstone carver's philosophy and attitude toward his profession, Hawthorne wrote that Wigglesworth seemed "to view mankind in no other relation than as people in want of tomb-stones." The tombstones above are now on the historical society's grounds in Edgartown.

ELDRIDGE'S FISH MARKET, FEBRUARY 1952

(**This page and left**) *Near the inn where Eisie was staying, he found these gulls screaming and swarming over a freshly shucked pile of scallops. Others perched patiently on the roof of Eldridge's fish market, hoping the boats would come in.*

The fish market, which is no longer there, was used in the winter for a shucking shed for the delicious scallop, harvested from mid-fall to early spring and an important part of the winter economy. The shells are often used to pave dirt roads and for garden paths.

MAIN STREET, EDGARTOWN, FEBRUARY 1952

In the winter, the island population drops from 65,000 to 12,000, and the towns seem to repossess themselves, regaining their individual characters. Town meeting controversies, holidays, and school affairs dominate the news. Most of Edgartown's stores close and the center of town is deserted in the evenings.

TOWN DOCK, FEBRUARY 1952

"It was in the office one day," Ralph Graves, nature editor for Life Magazine *at the time, recalls, "that Eisie and I discovered we both went to the island in the summer, and it would be fun to do a story for* Life *about a summer resort in the wintertime." Their superiors agreed, and Ralph, Eisie, and Kathy, Eisie's wife, arrived on the Vineyard on a bitterly cold day in February 1952. They stayed for a week at the Daggett House, an eighteenth-century inn on the waterfront adjacent to the town dock.*

They were greeted with a light snow that turned the island a winter white, accentuating the sculptural form of the old anchors from whaleships. At the far left is the lookout at the town dock, a vantage point from which Eisie has photographed the harbor many times.

HENRY BEETLE HOUGH, 1980

The late Henry Beetle Hough, author and owner and editor of the Vineyard Gazette *for forty-five years, on his daily walk with his collie. Witty and wise, a born philosopher, and distinguished conservationist, he was known as the "conscience of Martha's Vineyard." His dedication to preserving the natural beauty of the island was a lifelong crusade for which he gained a wide following.*

The Edgartown Lighthouse behind him is just one small example of his efforts to enhance the island's natural beauty. In 1935, the United States Coast Guard decided to remove the wooden building there serving as the lighthouse and replace it with a metal structure. On hearing this, Hough and his late wife, Betty, immediately began to search for a more aesthetically and historically suitable lighthouse, which they found in Ipswich, Massachusetts. They made the proper arrangements with government authorities, and it was brought down to Edgartown on a barge.

EDGARTOWN LIGHTHOUSE, 1973

*Alongside the walkway leading down to the Edgartown Lighthouse,
there is a beautiful hedge of rose of Sharon that bursts into bloom in
August. Eisie has photographed it several times, and on one occasion,
a tourist was there taking a picture of the scene. Knowing the results
would be disappointing, Eisie suggested to the stranger, "If you stand
a little further to the right, I think it'll be better." Visibly annoyed, the
tourist snapped, "Who do you think you are, Alfred Eisenstaedt?" and
walked off.*

*From this vantage point one can look out across the outer harbor to
Chappaquiddick Island in the distance.*

EDGARTOWN WATERFRONT, FEBRUARY 1952

In the 1950s, the shipyard on the Edgartown waterfront had space to store small boats for the winter, shown here covered with tarpaulin. The large double-chimney house in the background on the left is one of the most elegant in Edgartown. Known as the Bliss House or Captain's House, it was bought by Captain Jared Fisher, whose granddaughter would marry a Bliss. It remained in the same family until 1961, when it was taken over by the Society for the Preservation of New England Antiquities. In the summer, a mannequin of a woman stands on the rooftop lookout peering through a spyglass out to sea as if looking for her husband's whaleship.

MAYHEW BURIAL PLOT, EDGARTOWN, 1969

Descendants of the original white settlers are buried in this graveyard behind a house fronting on Edgartown Harbor (Chappaquiddick Island is in the background). It is believed that Governor Thomas Mayhew of Watertown, Massachusetts, who originally purchased the Vineyard, is also buried here along with members of his family.

MANUEL SWARTZ ROBERTS, FEBRUARY 1952

Manuel Swartz Roberts in his shop on the Edgartown waterfront. Island residents, summer people, and visiting yachtsmen all knew Manuel and hung around the shop chatting and watching him work with his uncanny expertise and artist's perception. Whether he was building one of his famous catboats, repairing a piece of furniture, or crafting something for a stranger who had sailed into Edgartown, it was done with extraordinary skill.

Manuel's shop, which has been the Old Sculpin Art Gallery since 1955, is right at the Chappaquiddick ferry dock, so he also ran the ferry. When the large bell on the Chappaquiddick side of the harbor rang, he would put aside his tools temporarily and go to pick up the passengers.

OLD SCULPIN ART GALLERY, EDGARTOWN, 1972

The only original building left on the Edgartown waterfront from the era of oar and sail, the gallery was the first on the island to sponsor summer lectures and other programs to raise money for the gallery's maintenance and for art programs for the island schools. For over twenty years, Eisie gave slide lectures for the gallery.

CHAPPAQUIDDICK

CHAPPAQUIDDICK FERRY, 1969

Chappaquiddick Island, which is the barrier enabling Edgartown to have its large, beautiful harbor, is reached by tiny ferries that jitney back and forth across the harbor's narrow neck. This photograph shows the two-car ferry crossing the harbor, with Chappaquiddick in the background.

Until about 1920, passengers were rowed across in a wooden skiff, and the fee was a few cents. Freight and cars were floated across on a barge. The first self-powered ferry was the City of Chappaquiddick, *and this was followed by the ferry* On Time I, *so named by the builder because he promised to have it finished on time for the upcoming summer season. Since then, there have been two more* On Times *running back and forth from dawn until midnight in the summer.*

CHAPPAQUIDDICK BEACH CLUB, 1968

When Edgartown first became a favorite summer resort, vacationers would sail over to this fine swimming beach to picnic and swim. In the 1960s, it became a private club. These colorful bathhouses line the shore, and it faces out toward Edgartown's outer harbor.

REGATTA, 1969

(Following overleaf) "There is nothing more exciting than to be well up in a big fleet of cruiser-racers, beating for the finish line in a hard sou'wester off Edgartown," yachtsman John Parkinson, Jr., wrote in The Bay and the Sound. *Photographing from the open deck above the town dock, Eisie caught a fleet of Rhodes 19s returning from a race with their spinnakers bellying out in a fair breeze.*

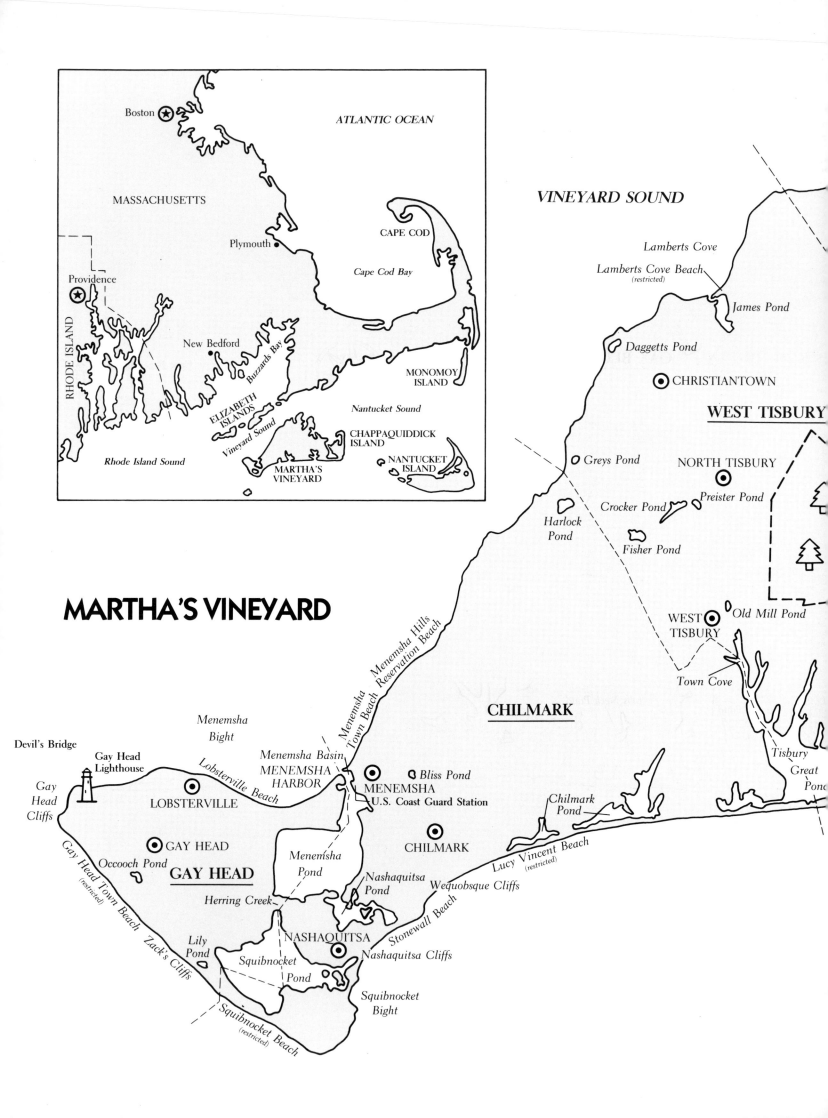

MARTHA'S VINEYARD

ATLANTIC OCEAN

Boston ★

MASSACHUSETTS

Plymouth •

CAPE COD

Cape Cod Bay

Providence ★

New Bedford •

RHODE ISLAND

Buzzards Bay

MONOMOY
ISLAND

Nantucket Sound

ELIZABETH
ISLANDS

CHAPPAQUIDDICK
ISLAND

Vineyard Sound

Rhode Island Sound

MARTHA'S
VINEYARD

NANTUCKET
ISLAND

VINEYARD SOUND

Lamberts Cove

Lamberts Cove Beach
(restricted)

James Pond

Daggetts Pond

⊙ CHRISTIANTOWN

WEST TISBURY

○ Greys Pond

NORTH TISBURY
⊙

Preister Pond

Crocker Pond

Harlock
Pond

Fisher Pond

Old Mill Pond

WEST
TISBURY ⊙

Town Cove

CHILMARK

Tisbury
Great
Pond

Menemsha Hills
Reservation Beach

Menemsha Town Beach

Menemsha
Bight

Devil's Bridge

Gay Head
Lighthouse

Menemsha Basin
MENEMSHA
HARBOR

⊙ Bliss Pond

Lobsterville Beach

MENEMSHA
U.S. Coast Guard Station

Chilmark
Pond

Gay
Head
Cliffs

LOBSTERVILLE ⊙

⊙ GAY HEAD

GAY HEAD

Occooch Pond

Menemsha
Pond

CHILMARK ⊙

Lucy Vincent Beach
(restricted)

Gay Head Town Beach
(restricted)

Herring Creek

Nashaquitsa
Pond

Wequobsque Cliffs

Zack's Cliffs

Lily
Pond

NASHAQUITSA ⊙

Stonewall Beach

Squibnocket
Pond

Nashaquitsa Cliffs

Squibnocket
Bight

Squibnocket Beach
(restricted)

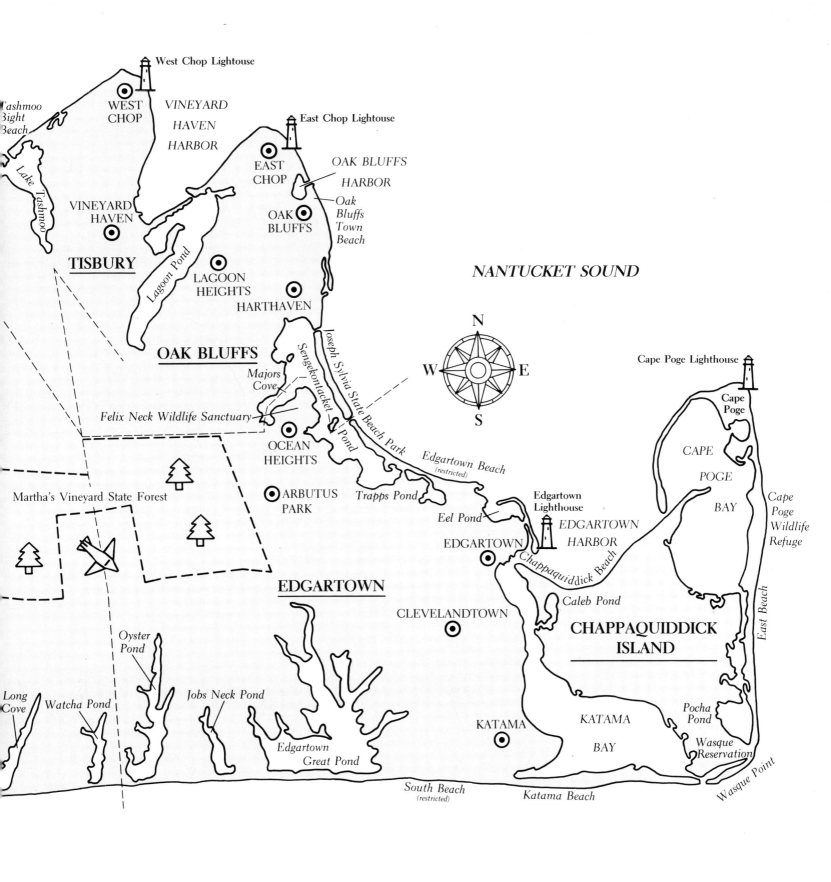

West Chop Lighthouse

WEST CHOP

Tashmoo Bight Beach

VINEYARD HAVEN HARBOR

East Chop Lighthouse

EAST CHOP

OAK BLUFFS HARBOR

Oak Bluffs Town Beach

NANTUCKET SOUND

Lake Tashmoo

VINEYARD HAVEN

OAK BLUFFS

TISBURY

LAGOON HEIGHTS

HARTHAVEN

Lagoon Pond

OAK BLUFFS

Majors Cove

Felix Neck Wildlife Sanctuary

OCEAN HEIGHTS

Sengekontacket Pond

Joseph Sylvia State Beach Park

Cape Poge Lighthouse

Cape Poge

CAPE POGE BAY

Cape Poge Wildlife Refuge

Martha's Vineyard State Forest

ARBUTUS PARK

Trapps Pond

Edgartown Beach (restricted)

Eel Pond

Edgartown Lighthouse

EDGARTOWN HARBOR

EDGARTOWN

Chappaquiddick Beach

East Beach

EDGARTOWN

Oyster Pond

Long Cove

Watcha Pond

Jobs Neck Pond

CLEVELANDTOWN

Caleb Pond

CHAPPAQUIDDICK ISLAND

Pocha Pond

Edgartown Great Pond

KATAMA

KATAMA BAY

Wasque Reservation

South Beach (restricted)

Katama Beach

Wasque Point

0   1 Mile

ATLANTIC OCEAN

Designed by Carol Middleton

Composition in Electra and Electra Cursive
with display in Kabel Demi by Media Services, Inc.
Birmingham, Alabama

Color separations by Capitol Engraving Company
Nashville, Tennessee

Printed and bound by Arcata Graphics
Kingsport, Tennessee

Text sheets are Lithofect by Miami Paper Company
Miami, Ohio

Endleaves are Rhododendron by Strathmore Paper Company
Westfield, Massachusetts

Cover material is Kingston Natural Finish
by The Holliston Mills, Inc.
Kingsport, Tennessee